PRINCEWILL LAGANG

Tesla's Titan: The Elon Musk Chronicles

First published by PRINCEWILL LAGANG 2023

Copyright © 2023 by Princewill Lagang

All rights reserved. No part of this publication may be reproduced, stored or transmitted in any form or by any means, electronic, mechanical, photocopying, recording, scanning, or otherwise without written permission from the publisher. It is illegal to copy this book, post it to a website, or distribute it by any other means without permission.

Princewill Lagang asserts the moral right to be identified as the author of this work.

First edition

This book was professionally typeset on Reedsy.
Find out more at reedsy.com

Contents

1. A Visionary's Genesis — 1
2. The Birth of Tesla — 4
3. The Solar Revolution — 7
4. The Autopilot Odyssey — 10
5. SpaceX and the Mars Odyssey — 13
6. The Hyperloop and Beyond — 16
7. Challenges and Controversies — 19
8. The Ongoing Vision — 22
9. Looking to the Future — 25
10. Legacy and Inspiration — 28
11. The Road Ahead — 31
12. A World Transformed — 34
13. Summary — 37

1

A Visionary's Genesis

"Tesla's Titan: The Elon Musk Chronicles"

The year was 1971, and a restless boy of just ten years old roamed the dusty streets of Pretoria, South Africa, his mind ablaze with curiosity and wonder. This boy, born on June 28, 1971, was Elon Reeve Musk. Little did the world know that this child's insatiable appetite for knowledge and an unwavering determination to change the world would one day shape the future of humanity.

From an early age, Elon displayed signs of exceptional intelligence and an intense desire to explore the mysteries of the universe. He voraciously devoured books, immersing himself in the works of Isaac Asimov, Arthur C. Clarke, and Douglas Adams, filling his young mind with dreams of space travel, artificial intelligence, and electric cars. His fascination with science and technology set him on a path that would ultimately lead to his ascent as a modern-day titan.

As Elon grew older, he faced a tumultuous childhood that would ultimately shape his character and fortify his resolve. His parents, Maye and Errol

Musk, were a study in contrast, with Maye being a passionate dietitian and model while Errol was an adventurous electromechanical engineer. This juxtaposition of his parents' influences would go on to profoundly affect Elon, fostering both an analytical mind and an unyielding ambition.

Elon's early education offered only a glimpse of his genius. At Waterkloof House Preparatory School, his peers often found themselves outclassed by his rapid comprehension and ability to solve complex problems with ease. It was clear that he was not your average schoolboy. However, life at school was not without its difficulties, as young Elon was frequently bullied, a hardship that he would later cite as instrumental in building his resilience.

The Musk family's move to Canada in 1989 marked a turning point in Elon's life. Just 17 years old and far from his homeland, he embarked on a journey that would eventually lead him to Silicon Valley, the epicenter of technological innovation. After completing his education in Canada, he chose to enroll at the University of Pennsylvania, where he majored in both economics and physics, a combination that would later serve as a solid foundation for his future endeavors.

While at university, Elon recognized the immense potential of the internet, even in its embryonic state. He co-founded Zip2, a company that provided business directories and maps for newspapers. The sale of Zip2 to Compaq in 1999 brought Elon his first taste of success, and he used the proceeds to co-found X.com, which would eventually become PayPal, revolutionizing online payments.

But Elon was far from satisfied. The nascent entrepreneur had bigger dreams, dreams that extended beyond online commerce. In 2002, he founded SpaceX, an aerospace manufacturer and space transportation company. Elon's ambitions for humanity were clear: he wanted to make life multi-planetary by colonizing Mars. This audacious goal was met with skepticism and doubt, but Elon's determination was unwavering. SpaceX's Falcon 1 launch in 2006 was a costly failure, but it only fueled his determination further.

Simultaneously, he turned his attention to the automotive industry, founding Tesla Motors in 2004. Elon's vision was to create electric vehicles that would revolutionize the way we think about transportation, making electric cars not only practical but desirable. The journey was fraught with challenges, from production woes to near bankruptcy, but Elon persevered.

In the chapters that follow, we will delve deeper into the life of this enigmatic visionary, exploring his triumphs and tribulations as he seeks to transform the world. We will witness the birth of the electric car revolution, the quest for sustainable energy, the colonization of Mars, and so much more. For Elon Musk is not just a man; he is a force of nature, a titan of industry, and a pioneer of our time. His story is one of relentless ambition, innovation, and the unwavering belief that humanity's destiny lies among the stars.

In "Tesla's Titan: The Elon Musk Chronicles," we will venture into the heart and mind of a man who dared to dream the impossible and, through sheer determination, made those dreams a reality.

2

The Birth of Tesla

As Elon Musk's journey through life continued, the story of Tesla, the company that would redefine the automotive industry, was unfolding. The early 2000s were a pivotal time for Musk, a period of relentless pursuit and audacious innovation. With SpaceX taking its first steps in the aerospace industry, Elon was about to embark on another ambitious venture, one that would forever change the way we think about electric cars.

In the early 2000s, electric cars were largely seen as quirky, niche vehicles, often limited by their range, charging infrastructure, and public perception. Elon, however, believed that electric vehicles held the key to a more sustainable future. He was determined to create electric cars that could not only match but surpass the performance and desirability of their gasoline-powered counterparts.

The journey began with the founding of Tesla Motors in 2004, with Martin Eberhard and Marc Tarpenning as Elon's initial partners. The name "Tesla" paid homage to Nikola Tesla, the brilliant inventor who had pioneered alternating current electricity, and it reflected Musk's aspirations to bring about a revolution in energy and transportation.

THE BIRTH OF TESLA

Elon joined Tesla shortly after its inception, investing $6.3 million of his own money and taking on the role of Chairman of the Board. His vision for Tesla was clear: to create a high-performance electric sports car that would shatter preconceived notions about electric vehicles.

The first fruit of Tesla's labor was the Tesla Roadster, a sleek and sporty electric car that could accelerate from 0 to 60 mph in just 3.7 seconds. It was a revelation. Gone were the days of sluggish and uninspiring electric vehicles. The Roadster combined the thrill of high-speed driving with the environmental benefits of electric propulsion. It quickly gained attention and accolades from the automotive world, proving that electric cars could be more than just eco-friendly; they could be exciting.

Yet, the path to success was strewn with obstacles. The development of the Roadster was fraught with technical challenges, from battery issues to production delays. Tesla's financial woes were exacerbated by the 2008 global financial crisis, pushing the company to the brink of bankruptcy. Elon, however, remained resolute. He injected millions of dollars of his own money into the company to keep it afloat and even borrowed funds against his personal assets.

His faith was not misplaced. In 2008, with a loan from the Department of Energy's Advanced Technology Vehicles Manufacturing program and successful rounds of fundraising, Tesla was able to overcome its financial hurdles. The Roadster, having captured the world's attention, was followed by the Model S, an all-electric luxury sedan that redefined the standards of electric vehicles.

The Model S was more than a car; it was a statement of Tesla's intent. With its cutting-edge technology, sleek design, and impressive performance, it marked a turning point in the auto industry. For the first time, electric vehicles were not merely an eco-friendly alternative; they were the embodiment of the future.

But Elon Musk's journey was far from over. In the chapters to come, we will witness the rise of Tesla as it conquers new frontiers in sustainable energy, autonomous driving, and global expansion. We will delve into the challenges, the triumphs, and the innovations that have made Tesla a symbol of modern innovation. Elon Musk's determination to reshape our world was not limited to electric vehicles; it extended to the very foundation of how we power our lives. Tesla was not just a car company; it was a company with a mission to change the world, and in doing so, Elon Musk became the driving force behind a new era of transportation and energy.

In "Tesla's Titan: The Elon Musk Chronicles," we will continue to explore the relentless ambition and innovation of a man who dared to challenge the status quo, revolutionizing industries and pushing the boundaries of what is possible.

3

The Solar Revolution

As Elon Musk's Tesla continued its journey of innovation and transformation in the world of electric vehicles, another major undertaking was brewing, one that sought to redefine the way we generate, store, and use energy. The stage was set for Musk to embark on a new mission: a solar revolution that aimed to make clean energy accessible to all.

Elon Musk had long been a proponent of sustainable energy solutions, and he saw an opportunity to address one of the world's most pressing issues—climate change. He believed that transitioning the world to renewable energy sources was not only necessary but also profitable.

In 2006, SolarCity was founded, an idea conceived by Elon's cousins, Lyndon and Peter Rive. Elon provided early funding and guidance, and the company quickly became the largest provider of solar power systems in the United States. SolarCity's mission was clear: to make solar energy affordable and accessible to homeowners, businesses, and municipalities.

The concept was simple but revolutionary: customers could have solar panels installed on their rooftops, generating clean energy and reducing their reliance on traditional fossil fuels. It was a vision of a decentralized, sustainable energy future where individuals and communities could harness the power of the sun.

In 2016, Tesla and SolarCity merged, forming a vertically integrated sustainable energy company. This allowed for the development of an ecosystem that encompassed electric vehicles, energy storage, and solar power. It was a strategic move aimed at creating a one-stop solution for sustainable living.

Tesla's solar endeavors expanded beyond solar panels. The company unveiled the Solar Roof, a groundbreaking innovation that integrated solar cells into traditional roofing materials. This allowed homeowners to generate electricity while maintaining the aesthetic appeal of their homes. The Solar Roof represented a seamless blending of form and function, and it promised to revolutionize the residential solar industry.

To complement solar power generation, Tesla introduced the Powerwall, a home battery system designed to store excess energy for use during peak demand or power outages. The Powerwall offered homeowners greater energy independence and a backup power source, further reducing reliance on traditional grid electricity.

Elon Musk's vision extended beyond individual homes. He also championed utility-scale renewable energy projects, such as the construction of the world's largest lithium-ion battery in South Australia. This project not only stabilized the region's energy grid but also demonstrated the potential of large-scale energy storage solutions.

Tesla's foray into energy extended to commercial applications as well. The Powerpack, a larger-scale battery system, was designed to help businesses and industries manage their energy consumption efficiently. Major companies, such as Amazon and Target, adopted Tesla's energy storage solutions to reduce their carbon footprint and lower their energy costs.

In addition to solar and energy storage, Tesla ventured into electric transportation beyond cars. The Tesla Semi, an all-electric heavy-duty truck, was unveiled in 2017. With its impressive range and low operating costs, it aimed to revolutionize the freight and logistics industry while reducing carbon emissions.

As we continue our journey through "Tesla's Titan: The Elon Musk Chronicles," we will explore the inexhaustible ambition of a man who sought to rewire the world with sustainable energy. Elon Musk's vision reached far beyond electric vehicles; it encompassed every facet of our lives, from the way we drive to how we power our homes and businesses. His relentless pursuit of a more sustainable future was a testament to his dedication to addressing the urgent challenges of our time.

In the coming chapters, we will witness the evolution of Tesla as it tackles new frontiers, from autonomous driving to space exploration. Elon Musk's journey is a testament to the power of visionary thinking and the relentless pursuit of innovation, and it continues to reshape the world as we know it.

4

The Autopilot Odyssey

As the 21st century unfolded, the world watched with anticipation as Elon Musk and Tesla continued to push the boundaries of innovation. Having reshaped the electric vehicle and sustainable energy landscapes, the next frontier was autonomous driving. Tesla's Autopilot, a visionary system that aimed to redefine the way we navigate our roads, was born.

Elon Musk's vision for autonomous driving was clear: to create a future where human drivers were no longer necessary, where cars could navigate themselves safely and efficiently. The journey toward achieving this vision began in earnest in 2014 when Tesla introduced the first generation of Autopilot hardware and software.

The Autopilot system was designed to assist drivers by taking over some driving tasks, such as adaptive cruise control, lane-keeping assistance, and even the ability to change lanes automatically when the driver initiated a turn signal. It was a glimpse into a future where vehicles could communicate with each other and their surroundings, reducing accidents and traffic congestion.

The introduction of Autopilot marked a significant leap forward in the development of self-driving technology. However, it was not without its challenges. Tesla's Autopilot system drew both praise and criticism. While some celebrated the increased safety and convenience it offered, others raised concerns about the limitations and the role of drivers in monitoring the system.

Autopilot's evolution continued with each subsequent software update, bringing new features and capabilities. Autosteer, for instance, allowed vehicles to navigate highways with minimal driver intervention. Summon, another feature, enabled cars to park themselves or pull out of parking spaces remotely, adding a new level of convenience to Tesla owners.

In 2020, Tesla introduced Full Self-Driving (FSD) Beta, an advanced version of its autonomous driving system that promised to handle complex city driving scenarios. While the system was still in beta testing and required driver supervision, it was a major step toward achieving full autonomy. Tesla was collecting vast amounts of data from its fleet of vehicles, refining its self-driving algorithms with each mile driven.

However, the path to fully autonomous vehicles was not without controversy and skepticism. Safety concerns, regulatory challenges, and the complexity of real-world driving scenarios all presented formidable obstacles. Critics questioned whether the technology was advancing too quickly and whether it could truly deliver on its promises.

Elon Musk remained undeterred, reiterating his commitment to making autonomous driving a reality. His vision extended to a future where people could summon their Tesla vehicles, send them on errands, or even participate in the Tesla Network, a ride-sharing platform that would enable Tesla owners to earn money by allowing their cars to work as autonomous taxis when not in use.

The journey toward autonomous driving was a reflection of Elon Musk's unwavering belief in the power of technology to transform the way we live. It was a vision of safer, more efficient transportation and the potential to reduce accidents caused by human error. As we delve deeper into "Tesla's Titan: The Elon Musk Chronicles," we will continue to follow the evolution of autonomous driving and the impact it has on our society, our cities, and our daily lives.

In the chapters to come, we will explore Elon Musk's audacious plans for space exploration, interplanetary colonization, and the dawn of the new space age. His relentless pursuit of innovation and his unyielding dedication to pushing the boundaries of what is possible continue to shape the world in profound and unexpected ways.

5

SpaceX and the Mars Odyssey

As Elon Musk's journey through the realms of innovation and transformation continued, he set his sights on the stars. SpaceX, the aerospace manufacturer and space transportation company he founded in 2002, was destined to become the catalyst for the next great leap in human exploration—colonizing Mars.

SpaceX's mission was audacious: to reduce the cost of space travel and make it possible for humans to become a multi-planetary species. Elon Musk's belief in the necessity of colonizing Mars was grounded in the understanding that the survival of humanity depended on having a backup plan beyond Earth.

SpaceX's early years were marked by monumental challenges. The first three launches of the Falcon 1 rocket ended in failure, pushing the company to the brink of bankruptcy. But Elon Musk's determination to reach orbit and eventually Mars was unwavering. The fourth launch, in 2008, was a success, marking a turning point for the company.

SpaceX continued to make history by being the first privately-funded company to send a spacecraft, the Dragon, to the International Space Station (ISS) in 2012. This achievement opened the doors to a new era of space exploration, one where private companies played a pivotal role alongside government agencies.

The development of the Falcon 9 rocket, known for its reusability, was another major milestone. Reusable rocket technology promised to dramatically reduce the cost of access to space, making ambitious goals like Mars colonization more feasible.

In 2015, SpaceX unveiled its most ambitious project yet: the Interplanetary Transport System (ITS), later renamed the BFR (Big Falcon Rocket). The BFR was a massive, fully reusable spacecraft designed to carry humans to Mars and beyond. With its colossal size and payload capacity, it represented a quantum leap in space exploration technology.

Elon Musk shared his vision of a Mars colony with a population of a million people, a vision grounded in the belief that a self-sustaining colony on the Red Planet could ensure the survival of humanity in the event of a catastrophe on Earth. SpaceX's Mars colonization plan was not just a dream; it was a detailed, long-term roadmap.

As SpaceX continued to make advancements in rocket technology and conduct successful missions, the Mars dream came closer to reality. The first step was to send an unmanned mission to Mars, the Mars Colonial Transporter (MCT), which later evolved into the Starship.

SpaceX's progress in rocket reusability was demonstrated with the repeated successful landings of Falcon 9 first stages and the development of the Falcon Heavy, the most powerful operational rocket in the world.

In 2020, SpaceX made history by launching astronauts to the ISS aboard the Crew Dragon spacecraft, marking the first time a privately-owned spacecraft carried humans into orbit.

The journey to Mars is ongoing, with SpaceX conducting multiple Starship prototype tests and aiming to send the first humans to Mars in the not-so-distant future. Elon Musk's vision of a multi-planetary civilization, while fraught with challenges and uncertainties, continues to inspire a new generation of space enthusiasts.

In the next chapters of "Tesla's Titan: The Elon Musk Chronicles," we will explore the broader implications of space exploration, the potential for scientific discoveries on Mars, and the profound impact of Elon Musk's SpaceX on the future of humanity and the cosmos.

6

The Hyperloop and Beyond

Elon Musk's unrelenting drive for innovation and transformative change extended well beyond the boundaries of the companies he had already established. The idea of the Hyperloop, a revolutionary mode of transportation, was a testament to Musk's creative vision and his desire to disrupt traditional industries.

The concept of the Hyperloop was first introduced to the public in 2013 through a white paper published by Musk himself. This high-speed, low-pressure transportation system was designed to propel passenger pods through a near-vacuum tube at incredible speeds, potentially exceeding 700 miles per hour (1,100 kilometers per hour). It promised to be not only the fastest mode of terrestrial transportation but also one of the most energy-efficient.

Musk saw the Hyperloop as a solution to the problems of traffic congestion and long-distance travel. It was envisioned as a game-changer for both regional and intercity transportation, reducing travel times and carbon emissions. The idea quickly captured the imagination of engineers, entrepreneurs, and innovators worldwide.

Recognizing the transformative potential of the Hyperloop, several startups and university teams embarked on the journey to turn Musk's vision into reality. Competitions were held, prototypes were developed, and designs were refined, all with the goal of bringing the Hyperloop to life.

Among the early pioneers was SpaceX, which hosted the annual Hyperloop Pod Competition, providing a platform for student and independent teams to test their Hyperloop pods on a specialized track. The competition not only fostered innovation but also brought together a community of like-minded individuals determined to make the Hyperloop a reality.

While progress has been made in developing and testing various Hyperloop concepts, the road to commercial implementation is long and challenging. The technical, regulatory, and financial hurdles are substantial. However, the impact of the Hyperloop goes beyond the technology itself—it represents a paradigm shift in transportation thinking.

Elon Musk's influence extended to other transformative concepts as well. The concept of the Neuralink Corporation, founded in 2016, was born out of Musk's fascination with the human brain and his concern about the future of artificial intelligence. Neuralink aimed to develop brain-computer interfaces (BCIs) that could enable direct communication between the human brain and machines. The potential applications ranged from medical treatments for neurological disorders to the enhancement of human cognition.

Musk's involvement in Neuralink was part of his broader concern about the future of technology and its impact on humanity. He saw the development of BCIs as a way to ensure that humans could remain competitive in an increasingly AI-driven world.

Additionally, Musk founded The Boring Company in 2016, an infrastructure and tunnel construction services company. The Boring Company's mission was to alleviate traffic congestion by developing underground transportation tunnels for electric vehicles, known as the Loop. Musk's idea was to create a network of high-speed, underground transportation routes to ease urban transportation woes.

The company made strides in its tunneling technology and completed several test tunnels, including the Loop system in Las Vegas. These projects aimed to demonstrate the feasibility and efficiency of underground transportation and to pave the way for similar systems in other cities.

Elon Musk's innovative ventures have consistently pushed the boundaries of what is possible, from revolutionizing transportation with the Hyperloop to exploring the potential of BCIs with Neuralink. His commitment to solving complex problems and addressing future challenges continues to shape the technological landscape.

In the subsequent chapters of "Tesla's Titan: The Elon Musk Chronicles," we will delve deeper into Musk's ongoing endeavors and their potential impact on various industries and society as a whole. Musk's relentless pursuit of transformation and progress knows no bounds, and the story of his life and work is far from complete.

7

Challenges and Controversies

Elon Musk's journey as a visionary and innovator has been marked not only by remarkable achievements but also by a fair share of challenges and controversies. In this chapter, we explore some of the key trials and tribulations that have defined his remarkable career.

1. Production Woes at Tesla: Tesla's ambitious goals often faced setbacks on the production front. The company's Model 3, touted as a more affordable electric car for the masses, struggled with production delays and quality control issues. Musk himself acknowledged the "production hell" the company went through in its quest to meet the high demand.

2. Lawsuits and SEC Settlement: Musk's social media activity, including tweets about Tesla's stock, led to legal troubles. In 2018, he faced a lawsuit by the U.S. Securities and Exchange Commission (SEC) for securities fraud over a tweet that claimed he had secured funding to take Tesla private. Musk settled with the SEC, agreeing to step down as Tesla's chairman and pay a fine.

3. Labor Concerns: Tesla faced criticism and legal action related to labor

conditions at its factories. Workers' rights and safety concerns raised questions about the company's treatment of employees.

4. Autonomous Driving Safety: Tesla's Autopilot system faced scrutiny after a series of accidents, some fatal, involving vehicles in Autopilot mode. Critics questioned the safety and public perception of autonomous driving technology.

5. Cryptocurrency Tweets: Elon Musk's influence extended to the world of cryptocurrencies, particularly Bitcoin and Dogecoin. His tweets and comments about these digital assets had a significant impact on their prices and market volatility, raising concerns about market manipulation.

6. Challenges at SpaceX: The ambitious goals of SpaceX have not been without their setbacks. Rocket launch failures, delays in the development of the Starship spacecraft, and the immense technical and financial challenges of sending humans to Mars have tested the company's resilience.

7. Controversial Statements and Social Media Presence: Musk's presence on social media platforms, particularly Twitter, has been both a source of fascination and concern. His unfiltered and sometimes controversial statements have garnered attention and, at times, sparked backlash.

8. Hyperloop and Infrastructure Hurdles: The development of the Hyperloop concept, while inspiring innovation, has faced skepticism, regulatory hurdles, and significant financial challenges. The vision of transforming transportation through underground tunnels with The Boring Company also raised questions about feasibility and environmental impact.

9. Ethical and Societal Concerns: Musk's foray into ventures like Neuralink, with its potential for brain-computer interfaces, has sparked ethical debates about privacy, security, and the implications of such technology on society.

CHALLENGES AND CONTROVERSIES

Despite these challenges and controversies, Elon Musk's ability to weather storms, adapt to criticism, and continue pursuing his transformative visions has been a defining feature of his career. The chapters that follow will delve into Musk's responses to these challenges and how they have shaped his ongoing quest to reshape industries and advance humanity into the future.

8

The Ongoing Vision

Elon Musk's life and work have been a testament to unyielding determination and relentless innovation. In this chapter, we explore the ongoing vision of a man who continues to push the boundaries of what is possible in an ever-changing world.

1. Tesla's Global Impact: Tesla's electric vehicles have disrupted the automotive industry, spurring a wave of electric car adoption across the globe. The company's expansion into new markets and its ongoing commitment to sustainability have cemented its role as a leader in the electric vehicle sector.

2. Sustainable Energy Ecosystem: Tesla's integration of solar power, energy storage, and electric vehicles has created a holistic approach to sustainable energy. With the growth of Tesla Energy products and solar installations, the company is playing a crucial role in reducing the world's reliance on fossil fuels.

3. SpaceX's Ambitious Goals: SpaceX's accomplishments in rocket reusability, coupled with its plans for Mars colonization, continue to capture the imagination of space enthusiasts. The successful crewed missions to the

International Space Station (ISS) mark a pivotal moment in the commercial space industry.

4. The Boring Company's Urban Tunnels: The Boring Company's efforts to develop underground transportation tunnels have the potential to alleviate traffic congestion in urban areas. Projects like the Las Vegas Loop showcase the company's progress in creating a new mode of efficient transportation.

5. Neuralink's Vision for the Brain: Neuralink's ongoing research into brain-computer interfaces holds the promise of breakthroughs in medical treatments and cognitive enhancements. However, the ethical, privacy, and security concerns surrounding this technology continue to be a subject of debate.

6. Hyperloop and Sustainable Transportation: The Hyperloop concept, despite its challenges, continues to inspire innovation and offers a glimpse of a high-speed, energy-efficient future for transportation. Several startups and teams worldwide are working on prototypes and feasibility studies.

7. Cryptocurrency and Market Impact: Elon Musk's influence on the cryptocurrency market persists, as his tweets and statements about Bitcoin, Dogecoin, and other digital assets continue to move markets and shape the conversation around the future of finance.

8. Musk's Leadership and Resilience: Elon Musk's leadership style, characterized by audacious goals, innovation, and the willingness to take on immense challenges, has reshaped industries and transformed the way we think about technology and transportation.

As we approach the present day, the world continues to watch in anticipation as Elon Musk's journey unfolds. His vision for a sustainable future, human exploration of space, and groundbreaking technology developments are reshaping our world in profound and unexpected ways.

In the chapters that follow, we will explore the ongoing impact of Musk's endeavors, including the latest developments, challenges, and his unrelenting pursuit of innovation. Elon Musk's legacy is still being written, and his story remains an inspiration to those who dare to dream and challenge the status quo.

9

Looking to the Future

As we venture further into Elon Musk's ongoing journey, it becomes clear that his vision for the future knows no bounds. With each passing year, Musk's ambitions continue to redefine industries and shape the trajectory of human progress. In this chapter, we explore some of the key projects and endeavors that hold the promise of transforming the world in the years to come.

1. Mars Colonization: SpaceX's mission to establish a self-sustaining human presence on Mars remains one of Elon Musk's most audacious goals. The development of the Starship spacecraft, with its immense payload capacity and reusability, paves the way for ambitious missions to the Red Planet. The first crewed mission to Mars, a potential reality in the coming decade, could mark a historic turning point in human space exploration.

2. Interstellar Travel: Musk's passion for space extends beyond Mars. The Starship's capabilities are not limited to our solar system; it holds the potential to facilitate interstellar travel, enabling humanity to explore other star systems in the future.

3. Supercharging Sustainable Energy: Tesla's ongoing work in sustainable energy continues to expand. The development of new electric vehicle models, advancements in battery technology, and the growth of Tesla Energy products signal a future where clean, renewable energy sources are the norm rather than the exception.

4. Hyperloop and High-Speed Transportation: While the Hyperloop concept faces challenges, ongoing research and development efforts, as well as feasibility studies in various regions, suggest that high-speed, energy-efficient transportation systems could become a reality in the coming decades, transforming the way we travel.

5. Neuralink and Brain-Computer Interfaces: Neuralink's ongoing research has the potential to revolutionize the treatment of neurological disorders, enhance human cognition, and change the way we interact with technology. The ethical and societal implications of brain-computer interfaces will continue to be at the forefront of discussions.

6. The Boring Company's Urban Tunnels: The development of underground transportation networks in urban areas holds the promise of easing traffic congestion and providing efficient, sustainable alternatives to traditional transportation methods.

7. Cryptocurrency and Finance: Elon Musk's influence on the cryptocurrency market remains a dynamic force. The impact of digital assets on the future of finance, and the role of Musk and other innovators in shaping this landscape, is a topic of ongoing interest.

8. Global Environmental Initiatives: Musk's commitment to addressing climate change and promoting sustainability extends to philanthropic efforts and global initiatives. Ongoing partnerships and contributions to environmental causes demonstrate his dedication to creating a more sustainable world.

LOOKING TO THE FUTURE

As we look to the future, one thing remains certain: Elon Musk's impact on technology, transportation, and space exploration will continue to shape the course of human history. His relentless pursuit of transformative innovation has not only challenged the status quo but has also inspired a new generation of visionaries and innovators to dream big and push the boundaries of what is possible.

In the chapters that follow, we will keep a watchful eye on the latest developments, challenges, and triumphs in Elon Musk's journey. His story is a testament to the power of vision, determination, and innovation, and it continues to unfold in remarkable ways.

10

Legacy and Inspiration

Elon Musk's journey, filled with remarkable achievements, audacious goals, and enduring innovations, has left an indelible mark on the world. As we reflect on his legacy and the inspiration he provides to current and future generations, it becomes clear that Musk's impact extends far beyond the companies and technologies he has created.

1. Transforming Industries: Musk's ventures have redefined entire industries. Tesla has revolutionized the automotive sector, promoting electric vehicles and sustainable energy. SpaceX has revitalized space exploration, ushering in the era of commercial spaceflight. His other projects, such as the Hyperloop and Neuralink, continue to inspire innovation.

2. Sustainable Future: Musk's commitment to sustainability and the environment has set a precedent for corporate responsibility. The transition to electric vehicles, solar power, and sustainable energy storage has become a global priority, partly due to Tesla's success.

3. Advancing Space Exploration: SpaceX's achievements in rocket reusability, affordable space access, and Mars colonization have reignited interest in space

exploration. The prospect of a multi-planetary future, though challenging, remains a testament to the boundless possibilities of human ambition.

4. Technological Pioneering: Musk's contributions to technology and engineering, from the development of the Tesla Model S to the Starship spacecraft, have pushed the boundaries of what is possible in their respective fields.

5. Inspirational Leadership: Musk's leadership style, characterized by ambitious goals and a willingness to take on significant challenges, has inspired countless individuals to pursue their passions, think big, and push the boundaries of innovation.

6. Global Impact: Musk's vision and projects have a global impact, influencing governments, businesses, and communities to embrace clean energy, space exploration, and high-speed transportation.

7. Entrepreneurial Spirit: Musk's journey from co-founding Zip2 to leading multiple groundbreaking companies underscores the importance of perseverance, risk-taking, and innovation in the entrepreneurial world.

8. Challenges and Resilience: Musk's ability to weather challenges, learn from setbacks, and adapt to criticism serves as a lesson in resilience. His tenacity in the face of adversity has been a defining feature of his career.

9. Ethical and Societal Questions: Musk's work in areas like Neuralink and brain-computer interfaces raises profound ethical, privacy, and security concerns. It underscores the importance of ongoing discussions about the responsible use of emerging technologies.

10. Ongoing Inspiration: Musk's story continues to inspire a new generation of innovators and visionaries who aspire to disrupt industries, address global challenges, and dream of a brighter future.

Elon Musk's legacy is far from complete, as he remains an active force in shaping the future. His vision, ambition, and the ongoing impact of his companies continue to be sources of inspiration for those who seek to create positive change in the world. As we move forward, we can look to Musk's journey as a testament to the power of visionary thinking and the enduring quest to advance humanity and the possibilities that lie ahead.

11

The Road Ahead

Elon Musk's journey, marked by groundbreaking innovations and audacious goals, continues to shape the future of technology, transportation, and space exploration. As we look to the road ahead, we can anticipate further transformation and ongoing impact in several key areas.

1. Space Exploration: SpaceX's vision of colonizing Mars and making space travel more accessible will remain a focal point. The development of the Starship spacecraft, along with planned missions to the Moon and beyond, will continue to push the boundaries of human exploration.

2. Electric Vehicles and Sustainable Energy: Tesla's efforts to advance electric vehicles, renewable energy, and energy storage solutions will shape the transition to a more sustainable and environmentally responsible future. New vehicle models and further expansion into global markets are expected.

3. Sustainable Transportation: The Hyperloop concept and The Boring Company's tunneling projects hold the potential to transform urban transportation, alleviating congestion and offering energy-efficient alternatives to

traditional transit systems.

4. Brain-Computer Interfaces: Neuralink's research into brain-computer interfaces may lead to breakthroughs in medical treatments, augmenting human cognition, and transforming the way we interact with technology. Ethical and regulatory considerations will play a significant role in the development of this technology.

5. Cryptocurrency and Finance: The influence of Elon Musk and other innovators on the cryptocurrency market is likely to continue. The evolution of digital assets, the impact on traditional finance, and the regulatory landscape will remain areas of interest.

6. Global Environmental Initiatives: Musk's commitment to addressing climate change and advancing sustainability extends to philanthropic efforts and partnerships with global organizations. The impact of these initiatives in combating environmental challenges will be closely watched.

7. Innovation and Inspiration: Elon Musk's journey serves as an enduring source of inspiration for aspiring entrepreneurs, innovators, and visionaries. His resilience, ambitious goals, and the ability to overcome challenges will continue to motivate others to pursue their passions and drive change.

8. Regulatory and Ethical Challenges: As Musk's projects continue to push technological boundaries, issues related to safety, ethics, privacy, and regulation will remain at the forefront of discussions.

9. Geopolitical and Economic Factors: Musk's global influence and his role in industries critical to national security, such as space exploration, may be influenced by geopolitical developments and economic factors.

10. Legacy and Impact: The long-term impact of Musk's work on industries, society, and the environment will become increasingly evident, defining his

legacy and the lasting change he has brought about.

As we venture into the future, one thing remains certain: Elon Musk's journey continues to be a testament to the boundless possibilities of human ambition and innovation. His story is a reminder that the road ahead is shaped by those who dare to dream, challenge the status quo, and strive to make a positive impact on the world.

12

A World Transformed

In this final chapter, we take a moment to reflect on the profound impact of Elon Musk's journey on the world as we know it. From sustainable energy and electric vehicles to space exploration and technological innovation, his vision and relentless pursuit of transformative change have reshaped industries, inspired countless individuals, and left an indelible mark on society.

1. Sustainable Future: Elon Musk's commitment to sustainable energy has accelerated the transition to a world where fossil fuels play a diminishing role. Tesla's electric vehicles and energy products have spurred a global shift toward cleaner, renewable energy sources.

2. Space Exploration: SpaceX's achievements in rocket reusability and affordable space access have rekindled humanity's passion for space exploration. The prospect of colonizing Mars and making space travel more accessible is no longer the stuff of science fiction.

3. Technological Advancements: Musk's projects, from the development of autonomous electric vehicles to brain-computer interfaces, have pushed

the boundaries of technology and engineering. They serve as a testament to the power of visionary thinking and the capacity of innovation to address pressing global challenges.

4. Transportation Revolution: The Hyperloop concept and The Boring Company's tunneling projects have the potential to revolutionize the way we travel, reducing traffic congestion and offering energy-efficient alternatives to traditional transit systems.

5. Global Inspiration: Elon Musk's journey continues to inspire individuals worldwide, from aspiring entrepreneurs to seasoned innovators. His resilience in the face of challenges, his unwavering ambition, and his capacity to transform industries motivate others to dream big and effect positive change.

6. Challenges and Ethical Questions: Musk's work has brought forth challenges, controversies, and ethical questions that society must grapple with. From the impact of autonomous driving to the ethical considerations of brain-computer interfaces, these discussions remain essential.

7. Environmental Responsibility: Musk's global initiatives and partnerships for environmental responsibility reflect a growing awareness of the need to address climate change and protect the planet for future generations.

8. Legacy and Ongoing Impact: Elon Musk's legacy is still being written, and the impact of his work on technology, transportation, and space exploration will continue to shape the course of human history. His vision, resilience, and capacity for innovation will remain sources of inspiration for generations to come.

As we conclude our exploration of Elon Musk's journey, we see a world that has been transformed by the power of visionary thinking and the relentless pursuit of innovation. Musk's story is a testament to the potential for individuals to challenge the status quo, advance humanity, and shape the world in ways that were once unimaginable. The road ahead is shaped by those who dare to dream, and Elon Musk's journey reminds us that the possibilities are boundless for those who seek to create positive change in the world.

13

Summary

"Tesla's Titan: The Elon Musk Chronicles" takes you on an in-depth journey through the life and work of Elon Musk, one of the most influential and visionary entrepreneurs of our time. In this extensive exploration, we have covered his significant contributions in various fields, including electric vehicles, sustainable energy, space exploration, transportation innovation, and brain-computer interfaces. The narrative has highlighted Musk's audacious goals, relentless pursuit of innovation, and unwavering commitment to addressing global challenges.

The book consists of twelve chapters, each focusing on a distinct phase of Musk's remarkable journey:

1. Introduction: Setting the stage for Elon Musk's journey and the impact he has had on our world.

2. The Solar Revolution: Musk's commitment to sustainable energy, the creation of Tesla, and the integration of solar power and energy storage.

3. The Autopilot Odyssey: Tesla's Autopilot system and Musk's vision for autonomous driving technology.

4. SpaceX and the Mars Odyssey: The founding of SpaceX, its accomplishments, and the audacious goal of colonizing Mars.

5. The Hyperloop and Beyond: Musk's vision for the Hyperloop and his ventures like Neuralink and The Boring Company.

6. The Ongoing Vision: A look at the ongoing projects and endeavors that continue to transform industries and reshape the future.

7. Challenges and Controversies: The obstacles and controversies Musk has faced in his career.

8. Legacy and Inspiration: The lasting impact of Musk's work on industries, society, and future generations.

9. Looking to the Future: A glimpse of what lies ahead, from Mars colonization to sustainable transportation and technology.

10. The Road Ahead: Reflections on the ongoing influence of Musk's ventures and his commitment to innovation.

11. A World Transformed: The profound impact of Musk's journey, from sustainable energy and space exploration to technological advancements and global inspiration.

12. Summary: A recap of the transformative journey of Elon Musk and the lasting legacy he leaves behind.

Elon Musk's life and work exemplify the power of visionary thinking, resilience in the face of challenges, and the capacity for innovation to shape the world. His legacy continues to inspire and guide individuals, businesses, and society toward a future defined by cleaner energy, sustainable transportation, and the boundless possibilities of space exploration and technology.